VOICE LESSONS

For Glenda,
whose company and whose music in story and song these two weeks at Wildacres have given me the pleasure of your voice. Thank you.
— Sue

July, 2001

Copyright 1998 Sue Lile Inman

Although sometimes in different versions, poems in this collection have appeared in the following publications:

The Devil's Millhopper: "Persephone"; *The Emrys Journal*: "Preserving the Reputation of Virgins," "The Tiresias Eye," "And There He Kept Her Very Well"; *Inside Out* (Cedar Mountain Press, 1986): "Something to Look For," "Swallows Along the Potomac," "A Child Remembered," "An Occasion," "A Summer Hike Not Far from the Chattooga," "Forty/Love: A Woman Looks Out Her Hospital Window," "Lines Carried by Wind," "Slow Circles," "October First," "Amaryllis in Winter Light," "My Mother's Wartime Transportation"; *The Kennesaw Review*: "The Woman Minister Preaches on Esau and Jacob," "Random Gifts"; *The Oconee Review*: "The Swimmer"; *The South Carolina Review*: "Something to Look For"; *Voices International*: "Slow Circles."

Grateful acknowledgment is made to the following for the use of copyrighted material: On page 11, for the quotation from "Too Young," words by Sylvia Dee, music by Sid Lippman. Copyright 1951; renewed 1979 Aria Music Co. Aria Corporation, Elkins, West Virginia. On page 42, for the quotation from "What'll I Do," words and music by Irving Berlin. Copyright 1924 The Estate of Irving Berlin, distributed by Hal Leonard Corporation, Milwaukee, Wisconsin.

The author would like to thank the women and men of the Emrys Foundation for fifteen years of continuous encouragement of creativity in the arts.

Library of Congress Catalog Card Number: 97-78039
ISBN 0-9645778-3-6

The Emrys Poetry Series

EDITORS

Keller Cushing Freeman
Jo Ann Walker

The Emrys Foundation
P. O. Box 8813
Greenville, South Carolina 29604

The Emrys Poetry Series

I. Jan Bailey, *Paper Clothes*, 1995
II. Marian Willard Blackwell, *Glassworks*, 1996
III. Becky Gould Gibson, *First Life*, 1997
IV. Sue Lile Inman, *Voice Lessons*, 1998

Cover design by Dawn Reese

Printed in Greenville, South Carolina, by A Press, 1998

The Emrys Press editors wish to acknowledge the help and encouragement of Gilbert Allen and William Rogers of Ninety-Six Press.

Voice Lessons

Sue Lile Inman
SUE LILE INMAN

Contents

My Mother's Remedies   5

One Match   7

My Mother's Wartime Transportation   8

Aunt Ocie Gave Herself Away   9

Lucky   11

A Child Remembered   12

In Praise of Sun   13

Voice Lesson   14

Preserving the Reputation of Virgins   16

Early Lessons in Marriage   17

The Internist's Assistant, 1959   19

The Tiresias Eye   21

October First   22

An Occasion   23

The Horticulturist Speaks   24

Slow Circles   25

A Summer Hike Not Far from the Chattooga   27

The Swimmer   28

Persephone   30

And There He Kept Her Very Well   31

Else   32

Something to Look For   33

The Woman Minister Preaches on Esau and Jacob   34

The Calling and the Practice: A Wedding Poem   35

Beneath the Lines: A Wedding Poem   *37*

Entropy   *38*

What Her Surgeon Could Have Said to Her Husband   *40*

Forty/Love: A Woman Looks Out Her Hospital Window   *41*

In Her Room   *42*

At the Cabin, One Last Time   *44*

Amaryllis in Winter Light   *45*

Random Gifts   *46*

Swallows Along the Potomac   *47*

Picnic Beside Lake Biwa   *48*

Winter in Nagahama   *50*

Obaasan (Old Grandmother)   *51*

Ways of Waiting   *52*

Lines Carried by Wind   *53*

What Is Held Back   *54*

A Story Is About Something   *55*

for Sam

My Mother's Remedies

Mercurochrome: the burning meant it was working;
rubbing alcohol cleaned away the germs;
Camphophenique: the smell alone oiled healing.

Calamine lotion for mosquito bites,
for chicken pox, chiggers; red whelps on thin
scratched legs creamed pink.

Milk of Magnesia: thick chalk poured
from a blue bottle. When I balked, she decreed:
This or an enema.

Some evil-smelling orange iridescent
glaze to stop us from sucking our thumbs.
I learned to peel it away just enough.

Mentholatum in a snug green jar for a stuffy nose.
Neosynephrine nose drops: when a sore throat
threatened to keep me from my cousins,

I treated myself, for a fast cure,
to a whole dropper-load, choked
and gagged my way to go.

Cod liver oil each morning: amber shining
from a silver demitasse spoon, washed
down with fresh-squeezed orange juice.

Gentian Violet for impetigo, caught in a sandbox.
We were painted purple,
around our mouths, on fingers, toes.

But what for burns? The sudden blue burst
when I tried to light the oven,
singeing eyelashes, brows, hairs on my arms.

The heat, the flesh-burnt odor, I remember.
But not the remedy. Warrior against hurts,
she would know what to do.

One Match

Those cold mornings before daylight,
I'd hear my mother engaged in a contest
to see if she could make it through the whole house,
lighting fires in gas heaters, room by room,
with a single kitchen match, and when she'd pass
through my room to the narrow hall, into the tile bath,
I'd hear her swear, the blackened match
burning so low it singed her fingers,
then with the study stove lit,
she'd open the door and hurry through the dining room,
kept closed off to conserve what warmth
we had, and I knew she'd made it back
to the kitchen when I heard the swinging
door creak and smelled bacon crackling,
heard the scraping of burnt toast.

My Mother's Wartime Transportation

became my first and only bicycle, a dirty rust brown,
too tall for me, the tires slim as she,
too thin to hold me steady. I learned to balance,
not to wobble. But terrified to press the brakes,
I'd jump off and run beside it, rather than risk a flip.

One day my brother on his birthday bike, low, shiny-red
with wide tires, and I on my hand-me-down
rode all the way to the pink pavement, Edgehill,
where the rich lived. We coasted and pedaled,
making up which movie stars we were, what horses
we were riding, when one of us remembered the time,
how far away from home. She'd be mad.

Going so fast, how to stop?
I jumped off, bent on running the bike to a stop,
took a graceless slide. Elbows, knees, hands, legs
scraped raw from the pavement, I walked home,
stiff and miserable. John pushed both our bikes.
Street burns taught me to apply brakes, to trust my vehicle,
however inadequate, if I am not to miss the ride.
The ride I will not give up.

Aunt Ocie Gave Herself Away

Aunt Ocie entered contests and won
cakes, toasters, refrigerators, and even
a thousand-dollar wardrobe, which she gave away.
Winning did not extend to husbands.

Harold was a gambler, whose old Ford
once caught on railroad tracks. After the collision,
and their divorce, she nursed him five years,
then took off for the city to work
as a public stenographer at the Francis Marion.
Their son Van shined shoes at the corner
of 6th and Louisiana, not a favored spot.

Later she gambled on marriage again.
Uncle Ken teased and joked. His mustache,
heavy breath made me shy away.
He sat in his undershirt at the white kitchen table
with a glass and bottle. "Here," he ordered,
"Drink this beer. Right now. While you're a child.
Then you'll always hate the stuff."

They kept moving to smaller houses.
One burned to the ground, and we gave them
a sofa from our playroom. To get to their last house,
out Highway 10, we had to walk in from the road
and ford a stream. A cottonmouth swayed
through the water, its head up like a turtle's.
My brother and I scrambled up the bank, armed
with shale to hurl our best skipping rocks
against danger. Our parents urged us on
through fields of goldenrod and gnats
to a small house in the clearing, built of stones.
The dark interior smelled of kerosene.
We sat outside to visit. Aunt Ocie's warm eyes
welcomed us all but lingered on my father,
the brother who accepted her without shame.

Later Aunt Ocie converted to the Roman Catholic Church.
"How could an intelligent woman like Ocie,"
my father would lament, "give away
the freedom of her mind?" She sent me a long handwritten
prayer that I read and reread to my record of *Clair de Lune*.
I puzzled over Aunt Ocie but never asked, "Did you win
what you wanted? Was it enough?"

Lucky

Our day-camp counselor shows us scars,
dozens of them on her brown legs and arms,
one beneath her shirt near the collarbone.

"I've been burned and cut but I'm here."
In our Brownie uniforms, we circle her, sitting
cross-legged to eat our bag lunches.

Each day I eat one whole tomato, ripe
and deep red, like an apple, not sliced up
for my sandwich. My father calls it a Love Apple.

"You know the song *Too Young*?" she asks.
"It's right. Be careful." She sings, *They tried to tell us
we're too young, too young to really be in love*.

"Don't fall too early for a man." We eye her scars.
"Just call me Lucky," she says. "I'm lucky to be alive."
One by one, we touch her arm, the shiny raised lines.

I bite into the plump tomato's taut skin,
with its just-right taste. Sweet tart
juice runs down my chin.

A Child Remembered

I snap off my mother's snake plant
      and fasten it back
           with a safety pin.
I defy her, give notice,
      demand a rebuke.

Why does she slide past
      with words disguised
           as gentleness?
"I wonder what happened to my snake plant."

Mother, why don't you get mad?
Not everything is smooth
           as you make it with your iron
           on my starched pinafore
or your hands firm on my hair.

Is such a cushion of niceness love?
      I squirm away before the pillow
           takes my air.

In Praise of Sun
for Gini

I see you as you were then,
sitting in an oversized
white Adirondack chair, pale thin hands
on each broad armrest,
your small face lifted to the sun.
You coolly disregard splinters, peeling
paint, mosquito bites while you bask
with the sure faith of tiger lilies
shadowing the sturdy fence.

These days you smoke outside
in all weather, sitting on a granite bench.
The dogs sniff out squirrels in long zigzags
among stiff, brown leaves. You rarely walk,
just sit, smoke, gaze at the fallen leaves
obscuring the surface of the pond,
wonder if the fish will make it
till spring. If hope endures as well as gold
and spotted *koi*, summer solstice
will find you in one-piece swimsuit, sandals,
with garden gloves, trowel, seedlings, peat moss,
edging toward perennial reunion.

Voice Lesson

For our third date, Edmund sat beside me
on the black piano bench to teach
me to sing. He on the bass side, I above
Middle-C. He sang *Beautiful Dreamer*
from deep inside his chest, a rich baritone.
He wanted to find my range. He played a phrase.
"Now you sing it," he said. I stalled.

I distracted him with a story
of how my first-grade teacher at Rosedale Gardens
lined us up to sing. "Someone is off-key,"
she declared, and divided us in half. One group sang,
then the other. She kept on until two remained.
I was chosen. "Fine. You just mouth
the words, don't really sing," she said. This to the girl who
sang to herself while she colored American flags,
trying to stay within the lines.

Edmund, more determined than ever, pressed on,
hammering out camp songs, old hymns and sheet
music he found inside the piano bench:
*The Caissons Go Rolling Along, Little
Brown Church in the Wildwood, Home
on the Range, Mighty Lak a Rose*. He sang,
I clapped, cheered him on, refused to open up.

His kind brown eyes turned black with intent;
a pulse in his temple kept time. He explained,
"Everyone is born with perfect pitch;
it's just a matter of listening." I nodded, gripped
the bench. He sang and played his way
through *Moon River*, his eyes on my lips, waiting.
Blue Moon, Wish You Were Here, Cole Porter tunes.

Now and then, in quavering thin notes that hugged
Middle-C, I joined in, careful to be covered by

the weight of his voice. No matter what the pitch
or the tempo, he could not touch
what held me in check. I would not
let go. After he left, I looked at the piano
bench. The black finish had puckered
to a perfect imprint where he'd sweated out my resistance.

Preserving the Reputation of Virgins

A gynecologist spoke to our senior class
in the biology lecture hall of the women's college.
It was April 1958, a time of spreading dogwoods in full array
and full skirts with petticoats and cinched waists, saddle oxfords
and bobby socks. In matters taken up in the back seats of cars,
the prevailing rule of thumb, to remain a nice girl, was
everything but . . . . The men, good sons of Christian folk,
scarcely made it back to their dorms, flushed and trembling
with their ideals intact, standards for marriage hurling them,
and us, to the altar.

The doctor spoke to us of contraceptives, favoring a circular cap
with a bendable rim, assuring us a high degree of protection.
He looked out over the young women, rubbed his hands, smiled,
and assured us that if we made appointments with him soon,
before graduation and our summer weddings, he could make us
comfortable for our wedding nights. We could tell our
future husbands and they would be relieved. He would save them
the awkward entry, the drops of blood.
We blushed and trusted him.

Groups would go by bus across Atlanta.
The knowledgeable receptionist filed away our faces
as we turned pages in *Ladies' Home Journal* or *McCall's*,
avoided conversation, except as each one came out,
we'd say, "Got your candy box?" A nervous smile,
the only reply. The uniformed woman would glance up,
call the next, and mark the score.

The metal table, fluorescent glare, shining stirrups,
the doctor's probing look, the nurse's knowing air,
my wincing and clinging to some remnant of childhood,
a faint wish to undo the fumbling past, did nothing
to produce one drop of blood. But I was fitted for my future
with secrets intact, a discreet white box in hand,
like a box of succulent sweets covered with dark chocolate.

Early Lessons in Marriage

I.

I watch a neighbor set the table,
take care of two toddlers,
wash curtains, hang them out,
cook supper while we talk.
"Where do you find the energy?"
"Oh, it's nothing," she says. "It'll grow
as you need it."
I go home and sleep.

II.

Betty and Jim next door
invite us for bridge.
I watch how they fight
over the lead,
what he should have bid,
how she should have answered.
"Three no trump was good enough,
you had to go for a Grand Slam."

Is this the hand I've dealt myself?
I pass.

III.

Before Perma-press, the stack of ironing grew:
sheets, blouses, shirts with French cuffs,
wedding linen—a tangle of guilt I hid as best I could.

My mother-in-law came and scooped it up,
hired a woman to iron it all.

"It's not that she's not
a good manager of my son's household,"
she declares to someone in my hearing.

So that's what I'm supposed to be?
I go back to the book I'm reading.

The Internist's Assistant, 1959

The offices are mine in the morning.
The reception room's quiet and dusty.
I tend to appointments, pay bills,
call in prescriptions to Barefoot and Tatum:
This is Mrs. Inman of Dr. Witten's office, and
the pharmacists laugh. I wonder why.
I'm serious about my new name.

Dr. Witten is serious about hats.
When a new one arrives, he calls me
to view the tweed wool with a bright
feather in the band. He gazes as if
he can taste its special flavor.

For lunch he has me bring him a carton
of chocolate milk and a pack of crackers.
That's all. I take my lunch downstairs
in the small City Hall café,
reading *Sons and Lovers*.
When I read C. S. Lewis's tale of Psyche,
I cry so hard back in the lab
the doctor thinks he's said
something to hurt me. He's puzzled
I'm so serious about books.

The lab is narrow as a walk-in closet.
I peer into the microscope and count blood cells,
mark the score, count again, put test tubes
in the centrifuge, run urinalyses, soak another pair
of rubber gloves in cyanide solution, careful
to use tongs, prepare the dry ones for the doctor.

Emma Wilcox comes in for her weekly B-12,
the alcohol-soaked cotton comes off
her dark arm black. She pays religiously
the three dollars she believes is due.

The beautiful Cuban woman's next;
escaped Castro just in time, she tells me.
Her French perfume stays with us
all afternoon. Mrs. Nix lies on her right side
and I paint her ribcage first with alcohol,
beginning at the spot he shows me
in overlapping concentric circles; then in
orange-red iodine, I make a large germ-free target.
I stand beside her as he aspirates her lung,
the needle a serious four inches long.

He takes his time with each one;
in his office they talk, he listens.
I fidget at my desk; everyone has to wait.
He's told me not to worry. He learned
while he was sick with tuberculosis
to move at a pace that doesn't rush
a necessary process. He's told me his
patients count on his serious attention.

He likes his life and plans to practice
in his fashion until he's eighty.
His wallet bulges with cash and checks
he forgets to deposit. At the end of the day
he calls me into his office to tell
a difficult diagnosis he's made
that everyone else has missed.

I leave between six-thirty and seven
to meet Sam at the cafeteria.
My uniform is beginning
to bulge seriously at the waist. I'll work
until late fall, then give notice.

The Tiresias Eye

He sits in the center of the floor
in *The Waste Land*. Or you can see
him seated in front of the shoe store

at the mall. The blind prophet of Thebes
foresuffers all, or so he claims,
and no wonder: he's been both, grieves

both man and woman, consigned now to name,
like an artist who understands, with negative
capability, your point of view and mine.

Once he saw Athena bathing. She took
away his ordinary vision, replacing it, without
remorse, with this cruel joke:

He prophesies. Some say he mutters or shouts
nonsense. They drop coins in his guitar case, hope he'll
move on. Yesterday, I heard him sing out:

Why do you climb the ladder in high heels?
When you make love, do you close your eyes?
Has anyone painted portraits in blood?

A staining pigment in good supply.
Who is that caught now in their crosshairs?
When you dance for the rulers, watch what you buy.

For your paintbrush, use your own cut-off braids.
Healing comes only when a pure fool appears
to ask revealing questions with the artist's steady gaze.

October First

Do you see what's happening?
Do you see them,
monarchs flying at tree level?
Every day they leave customary flowers,
rise, and soon they'll meet
to make their descent into Mexico.

The lake's too dry for boats now,
its banks lie open like a hideous wound.
Hills yellow with goldenrod.
Sumac crescents sway on bare sticks.
Sourwoods deepen to burnt sienna,
their tassels bending to change.

Tell me you see.
Let the old insistent message pierce
your nostrils like ragweed, the incessant buzz
of locusts sound the alarm.
Highway mowers—they will warn you if nothing else—
lay waste kudzu and morning glories alike.

All yield the acrid scent,
chafe you with the knowledge:
Time is nearly up.
Let us rise and meet.

An Occasion

For the fiftieth anniversary of his birth,
a man deserves at least a tree.
If not, then what? A poem?
A song of jokes and brittle mirth
to hold off the heavy stone,
toss it like a Frisbee across the grass, desert, out to sea?

When it returns, I'll catch the stone, again
swing, and, throwing like a boy, skip it
across the night sky,
smash it, like a key lime pie,
on the moon's face.

The pied moon forever
a defiance to celebrate your stubborn birth.

The Horticulturist Speaks

I favor bow ties and suspenders
with a crisp white shirt of fine cotton
for my lectures to the ladies. My specialty,
perennial gardens. Despite Carolina humidity,
we stand in the sun and discuss placement of thyme,
basil, rosemary, fennel along the bank of poor soil,
how herbs thrive on neglect. I move toward shade,
point out how uplighting shows off
crape myrtle's sculptural effects: no need
for Cupid pouring water here. The ladies titter
beneath their hats. I pinch wilting petals
from purple cone flowers and call attention
to saucy orange butterfly weed below
for complementary balance. Never once do I
let my mind drift to Taos, and the handsome
nurse with calling eyes grieving his dead lover.

My skin is tan and I am fit
and mean to last. Tonight I shall bring up
the night-blooming cereus from my greenhouse,
pour my best bourbon, watch for the magnificent white flower.
I will not miss this one night of splendor.

Slow Circles

After twenty years a friend
meets my plane,
drives me through snow,
and we talk over coffee,
apple pie and hot cheese.

He listens with the quality
of holding
I had forgotten.
His face attends.
The pleasure so astounds me
I forget my words,
skip around, scatter my life
like pages in the wind,
embarrassed as a woman,
carrying too many packages,
who fumbles for her keys
in a cluttered pocketbook.

With the kind of tending
we seek in a physician,
he plans a better place
for unfolding history:

A picnic at Pinnacle
with only Methodists nearby.
His wife has packed it for us
at his request.
The deviled eggs she made with care,
thus presenting herself to me,
one of the smartest things
I've known a woman to do.

A mountain conversation
under scrub oaks, with birds

calling out after rain. We wedge
ourselves among the rocks
and spread our stories out.

A Summer Hike Not Far from the Chattooga

I.

A turn in the path, a winding down
into a sea of ferns and old trunks
draped in moss. The pool is near.
Laurel trunks lean and twist,
a pattern of antique mystery,
along the edge where springs feed
the clear deep pool, dark leaves give off
sharp spice. Stones, like guardians,
space themselves. Pebbles, smooth or jagged,
make way for her bare feet.
She sings as she peels off her sweaty clothes.

II.

He's never thought of himself
as a voyeur. But suddenly, rounding a turn
in the mountain path, having climbed over
tree trunk, around rocks, he sees her—
off to his left in a sheltered pool. Trees frame her
as if she were bathing in a house, he outside looking into her
        window.
He feels his face flush, tries to turn away.

III.

She watches her arms and legs turn golden as she sinks,
moves to find smooth stone, stretches. Flecks of sand
swirl, sparkle in the changing light. Silver, mauve, and white
rocks, like creatures, spread distinct, amaze her with their
        clarity.
She knows the pool to be hers, shared
only with minnows, crayfish, and spiders skating the surface.
The edge is safe, the deep is safe.
Her body eases. She's alone in her element.

The Swimmer

1.

The sculpture—seven feet long—
lies in a grassy pool, one arm reaching,
the other back, elbow poised like a wing,
legs in mid-kick, face intent.
The town's gold medalist swimming the grass,
her breasts nestled there.

A painter sets up his easel in the park,
between spring rains, paints the stone swimmer.
A photographer is eating his lunch
on a bench, sees the two of them:
the painter of New Realism and the sculpture.
He leaves his ham sandwich,
jogs back to his office for his Nikon.
First in black and white, later in Kodacolor ASA 400,
he catches what he wants: the real
sculpture, the canvas called The New Woman,
in flesh tones to look less grainy gray, more human,
and the painter. The next Wednesday, he
carries his camera and tripod. As he finishes his sandwich
and bites into a Winesap, noting it's too flat on one side
to be a real apple shape, he sees a boy in a sailor suit
climb onto the swimmer. Astride her strong back,
the boy waves his hat, calls out that he's riding a porpoise
out to sea, far away from his near-sighted sitter.
The photographer catches them in color,
though black and white would be more permanent:
the boy on his porpoise, the swimmer in the grass,
the painter with his hands on his hips,
the canvas woman in gleaming acrylics.

2.

She swims during her lunch break.
After ninety-five laps, she dries her buzzing legs,
remembering the reverie: she's been at her grandfather's,
pumping water out of the rusty pump,
up, down, up, down, then drinking from the bent cup,
copper-tasting, cold.
The part she likes best about swimming is the reverie.

Lights around the pool, the people, all an aura.
She showers off the chlorine, dries,
blow-dries her short hair, touches the gold
earrings still plugged in, slips on her clothes,
puts in her contacts. At the door of the Y,
she stops. For the first time, she feels a quickening,
like a small fish flipping over inside her. Soon she'll
shorten her laps. She smiles, intent on the hope she carries.

Persephone

He senses the wall of coldness and you behind it
wrapped in your cloak, puzzles over why you sit
content by the hearth of your own unknowing.

He thinks to woo you home by jewels from beneath
the earth, gifts only such a lord can bring;
calculates through a trick of clothing

to transform you. Hopeful as a boy, he opens
his eyes on nothing until you have changed
into the goddess he wed and means to keep.

You know what he is doing, and wait unmoved.
Musky secrets from his realm draw you back,
for a season. Your lips remember, belly remembers

pungent sweetness, pomegranates you have eaten
from his hand. He claims you have at last come
to your senses, this moist bed, this warm dark

where you belong. You hear your sisters singing
in your winter sleep: Artemis calls you
to the hunt; Athena's eyes hold you with the truth

of your undoing. You wake, believing one
solitary walk at night with only bats
and toads about will surely lead you home again.

And There He Kept Her Very Well
in response to Elena Sisto's Get Lost

Until she took a notion
to take up her pad and pen,
she was cute as a button. *Button,
button, who's got the button, now?*

The house is his, make no
mistake. See the tin man's
shadow on the ground?
He kept her buttoned up

until she held a flashlight
in his face, drew in
a breath at what she saw
and drew him just like that.

No wonder her hand shook
hot wax on his cheek.
In the flickering light
buttons flew in all directions.

He used to say, you
can depend on me, oh yes.
Hang yourself
on me, but not too close.

She flipped her hormones
and dared to laugh. We're comely,
you and I, and grotesque, she cried.
She's banished from his palace.

Pushpins hold up his notion
of her. She's stepping out
of the frame in one direction
or another. Now there's a chance.

Else

*"Night is longing, longing, longing
beyond all endurance."*
—Henry Miller

No, I will not allow such
a waste of time when you could be dead
to the world and dreaming.
If you allow yourself to indulge
in that kind of heart-churning,
barefoot-yearning,
throat-aching, belly-knotting
eye hunger
for one
living else-
where, probably sleeping,
tossing someone else's
heart upside down and backward,
what good can you accomplish?
What does it profit? I ask you.
Where is it written, you have to
spend every blessed moon-filled,
lilac-scented, boulder-strewn,
wild iris-patterned June
night of no sleep
with longing? I ask you,
where?

Something to Look For

None of these lines I send is exactly where I am—
I am feeling after you. It is dark here where you were
and has a peculiar odor, not frankincense,
unholy, like an earthly burning of bone and hair.

Not yearning, but a recurring wistfulness I know;
as when a child lulled by the car's motion drifts
softly in and out of sleep, hearing the grown-ups'
reassuring dull talk, then comes alert when they whisper.

Something important has been missed. I had intended to listen.
Now, patient as a dog, I circumscribe my life with layers
of obligation, taking, easily distracted, each one who beckons
as divine call and fair. Something close and obvious

eludes me. I would call your name if I could see exactly
who you are or were before I lost touch and now must catch at hints,
like the seekers on Sunday mornings who walk the landfill, casting
their sensitive wands for metal over glinting shards.

Can neglect accomplish such a burning? I find only smoldering
remnants of one whose passion once drew me out of sleep,
as when windows can at last be opened to spring smells,
and wisteria tugs the child to play beneath its honeyed vines.

The Woman Minister Preaches on Esau and Jacob
for Susie

She smiles from the pulpit, black robe and dark
hair marking off the white face. She speaks
the word as she receives it, not grimly.
In light charges, she makes her way
through the ancient text, her upcountry
nasal pitch notwithstanding.
In twin selves warring inside one woman
with power to create two nations, she finds
humor, pathos, irony, God's will.

She holds my gaze
on a God in the midst of conflict,
on Haitians singing *Amazing Grace* in Creole,
thin children who wiped away her tears
as she listened to their affirmations.
I go dizzy from looking her way.
Light charges and I go dizzy,
the way you do from looking hard into a snowbank
and then you go inside and cannot see.

In the vestibule, we speak cordially.
Fragrant, she gives a hug,
her breath charged with peppermint.
Set right again, I watch her face.
Still smiling, she reaches up,
laughs, removes her mask,
the white mask I saw in the pulpit.
Underneath—I go dizzy—she
wears the same face she took off.

The Calling and the Practice: A Wedding Poem
   for John and Amy

Confined by skin to live and walk alone,
as we are, and in due course to die that way,
we know or sense a pulsing near our bones
that calls us to a dance of longing for the day-
soul to complement our own night songs.

Is she the one? Is he? For years our silent refrain's
strummed out by crickets trilling beneath the window,
by elephants miles apart on the Serengeti Plain
rumbling to each other of love, or new routes to water,
in tones so deep no human ear detects the sound.

Whether by something of a lofty nature,
or mere pheromones, who knows? We're scanning
with more than our bodies, when, with a start,
we meet the one and see the future
shimmer and clarify: we commit our hearts.

This calling may be universal;
how we answer is our own to be done.
Like yoga, piano, writing, medicine, prayer,
marriage can be a practice, daily rehearsal
for making intentions and actions one.

It's a dance that keeps on changing, over time.
We learn the steps, point, counterpoint, and turn,
listen to each other's faces to make the cadence rhyme.
The focus it requires is like looking for a comet
from the corner of your eye. Mostly, we improvise.

The joy and delight arise from crossing boundaries
subtle as the thinnest membrane where spirit meets
spirit in the dancing air. A wise man once told me
how close you ever grow to your beloved,
there is an inmost room which only God can enter.

His words helped me trust in a kind of center
where each partner has a sacred space to renew and grow.
May your life together be a calling and a practice
of love that brings a healing touch to all you know.

Beneath the Lines: A Wedding Poem
for Bill and Karen

Beneath traffic, sirens, and busy signals,
voice mail, exhaust fumes, incessant commerce;
beneath the aromas of coffee, pesto,
oranges, summer rain on hot pavement;
beneath fog lingering over the river, sudden light on yellow roses,
the thock-pock of tennis balls on clay courts, the roars
and screeches from Washington Park Zoo;
beneath the snows on Mt. St. Helen's, Bachelor,
Broken Top, Rainier, Baker, Mt. Hood;
beneath currents of silence, in the still white empty places,
there is something eternal, a hum.

We stand with you today and pledge again
to listen, to learn by heart the steady hum of love
that keeps us all, infuses you with green
promise to make of life a unity of love,
generous as the vista from the mountain,
intricate as the smallest moth hidden in a sequoia,
strong as jonquils pushing up through asphalt,
familiar as your hands, daily as toast.
What you have and give one another rises
from this presence humming through our world:
God's grace, here, transparent, and enough.

Entropy

Remember the hike above Lake Lucerne?
How you marched on ahead as usual,
this time up the steep path at Birkenstock.
Beside a small chapel, a bronze nude sculpture
compelled me to stop: the young woman,
her face lifted, ecstatic with life,
dancing for all she's worth,
linked arm-in-arm at the elbows
arched back-to-back
with a partner she cannot see—
Death with his toothy grin.
I had no camera that day to record
this *Danse Macabre*, and could not
find the sculptor's name.
I ran to catch up, but
you'd had enough
hiking high with no guard rail.
We descended by cable car
through heavy fog so separating
we might as well have been alone.

It's what we practice that shapes
and divides us—
what we eat and where we live,
what we refuse to do or see;
where our minds go while we drive.
Time's missile homes in—
inevitable as rust on black deck chairs,
inscrutable as dust under the bed. Unspoken
assumptions rule our hearts and give order
to our days whether we examine our lives
or not. How about this one?
No law of thermodynamics
would dare interfere with the forward
thrust of our dreams and goodwill.
You buy me sequined dresses and high heels;

I suck in, girdle up, and smile
through reconstructed teeth. We walk out
onto the dance floor for all we're worth—
the exception, you and I.

What Her Surgeon Could Have Said to Her Husband

She may change. You must see that about her.
See her scars under lamplight, without flinching.
No absolute guidelines pertain for women
after breast cancer. Mysteries of hope
defy all medical predictions.
Anyone's loss, her loss of a breast, distills
belief. The progression of dreams
undermines all compassionate warnings.
She has it in her to be a cosmos
or yeast in bread braided with butter and honey.
She may become mist over the lake
scumbled by morning sun, or a teacup
warmer than the hands that protect it.
She may become a mother. She may leave.

Forty/Love: A Woman Looks Out Her Hospital Window

Take him
to your tight breasts

with your crisp assurance,
your backhand still strong,

a return he can count on.
Take him,

I don't want him
to see me like this.

Like that vacant lot
once a meadow, then plowed,

raked, farmed,
now overgrown by weeds,

in winter a tangle of gray tubes.
I suppose a refuge for small creatures,

those who fly or scurry.
Not man. His feet seek

open courts. Take him there
away from amber eyes

fixing him to the night,
away from this ruined land

he once called home.

In Her Room

The less people listen to her talk it out,
the more they turn away and keep on speaking,
the more she smiles and keeps silent in her room.
Rosehips sway on their spindly branches,
thorns curved rigid along the stems.
She does not dress till noon. Beneath her
full-length robe, rancid odors bloom.

At four o'clock a line of sun streaks the street
beyond the lawn. She brews a cup of herbal tea,
takes heart and begins a note:
I call that the line of hope, she says.
The weeping cherry shines silver—bark and branches—
in the winter light. The mockingbird likes it right well.
What can I say to you I haven't said before?
You are my son and I love you,
but you are far away. I drift farther still.
When we talk, it helps. We talk seldom now.
I will not call out
and bother you so many miles away.
The intercom between our rooms
does not extend that far.
I can no longer remember
what I hoped for.

She doodles down the sides of
the blue paper. A clown, a horse,
a tall pine tree. She sips her red tea and hums,
recalls the Asian pears drying on the windowsill,
shriveled now—individual as old friends—
and rises from her chair to draw them. Her left hip
calls out as she pushes up, but she is humming now:
What'll I do when you are far away?
Consigned to cheerfulness once more, she lets go—
the blue note drifts to the floor. The scent of turpentine

invites her to the worn palette—crimson, cerulean, ocher,
cadmium yellow light—rich colors of possibility.
She takes note and turns to paint.

At the Cabin, One Last Time

So what can I do
in the time left here?
Sit on the porch,
watch twilight change
gold sky to yellow cream,
watch color drain
from flame azalea.
Hemlocks deepen;
the greens, so varied in daylight,
of poplar, oak, pine, willow,
blue spruce blend, their distinct hues
swallowed by night shade.
From the eaves, bats take off.
Birds subside.
The woods are dark,
and now the porch.
The sky's still light;
night travels from the ground up.
The stream splashes on
like distant steady rain.
One lone bird calls out:
I'm here, I'm here.

Amaryllis in Winter Light

Beside this particular window, translucent
with dust and soot and winter light,
stands the amaryllis,
naked stalk, aggressive and erect,
blossoms in full white eloquence
drawing me to attention
as music from a closed room
provokes the mind
to piece together broken phrases.
So I contemplate this immigrant
refusing winter hugely,
wonder at its power
to declare I am
both male and female,
held in elegant poise
on a stalk that does not topple,
does not collapse, but stands,
inclines in a slight turn
toward the light,
mute and oblique as meaning.
Before the amaryllis charmed me,
anarchy held sway: briars and burdock
sprawled over paths to cling and tear,
forcing attention to scratches,
away from deeper wounds.
Its silent persistence daily upward
spears the brambled air
until mind-weeds dissolve.
Infinitesimal particles cluster
to make the glistening white bell
sound a steadying chord for me.
No abstract meaning here;
instead, a particular amaryllis,
envoy of the earth.

Random Gifts

Words, like ashes from trash burning,
float down through sunlight,
each a small boat, rose-colored, shaped
to hold one passenger, arriving silently
beyond the fence. Years ago what I pretended
were fairies floating down, now descend
as words for reckoning: *reach, day,
silhouette, murmur*. I run
to pick them up. My dog yelps and darts
from one to another. Her mouth full of words,
she wags her tail and drops them at my feet:
wind, star, pomegranate, edge, stone.
Each feels damp, rose-petal cool, a wafer,
delicate as a blessing, to take and eat.

Swallows Along the Potomac

What faith it must take to fly
like swallows by the river:
they drop like kami-
kazes, swoop, flick
to another direction, flash
their forked tails like signal
flags, graze buildings
with élan, skirt disaster with breathless
ease. It's all so easy to see—
they don't think, merely
trust themselves to the wind.

Picnic Beside Lake Biwa

It's a balancing act like walking
the curb: on one side traffic splashing
muddy water; on the other, dark-haired students
in blue-black uniforms bicycling to school,
with bookbags and clear plastic umbrellas,
a pack of giggles and averted eyes.
Aside from Japanese language class,
something waits for me,
displaced for now by this new work
to break the code, to speak and understand
staccato tongue-twisters overheard on the bus.

Follow Basho's journey perhaps: travel light
with paper, brush, and ink. Walk the narrow path
steep as the one we climbed to forty-eight waterfalls.
Remember the red maples, yellow gingko,
how they sprinkled the dark crevasse with light,
even hope. Remember how you wanted to linger along the boulders,
but we had to stay with the group, keep climbing
single file to one more sight.

Still something waits
to be talked out: what you want, what I want.
We sit without words and ponder how light
splashes the lake with gold, a path beyond
those dipping willows, a direct line to
mountains over there, tugging at us both
in separate ways, to leave
this gray square blanket with our simple picnic
and run speechless after the promise.

The trick of balance
must be somewhere: to sit still,
listen for the source of light,
make a home for it here in my belly.
I'll eat my fill, let autumn course through

my feet, legs, arms, and out my fingers.
By spring, surely I'll know what to do,
what to say, how to say it. I'll paint Japanese kanji
on large square sheets, centered and very black.
For you, for me, a stillpoint in a foreign tongue.

Winter in Nagahama

I

In snow deep as the evening bath
blackbirds probe pale cabbage.
A farmer's glove on a green stake
points stiffly to the hidden sun.

II

Strong winds off Lake Biwa
clothe the bronze nude by city hall
in white apron and cap. My coat
flies open.

III

From the rice field's ice mirror,
blackbird *karasu* tilts its head
to admire the black beak of the one
looking down. Tonight in Silk Road Bar
Kanemura will sit alone, sing karaoke
to the woman on the screen.

IV

This morning the crunch of fresh snow
sends memories up my legs:
of home, our walks, your hands.

Obaasan (Old Grandmother)

Every day I push my cart
to the garden behind my son's house,
hoe vegetables, pull *daikon*,
curse blackbird *karasu*, gather flowers.
Today I put in seventy-seven strawberry plants,
picked a bundle of daisies white and yellow
for Keiko-chan whose husband lies in the hospital.
Both very young and she pregnant with their first.

Tonight under the old moon, I made a plan.
I shall travel the pilgrim's road,
leave off sunbonnet, heavy boots, soiled apron,
wear white from crown to sole, prayer beads on my arm.
With book and bell, I shall climb with other pilgrims
to thirty-three holy places in Kansai.
Meet me on the boat to Chikubushima.
We'll make our prayers to the goddess and sing.

Ways of Waiting

There are hundreds of ways to wait,
good intentions unfulfilled, all of them blue.
A figure beckons from the spirit gate.

Needlepoint rugs, file your nails, watch debates
on TV, catalog the silver, polish shoes—
there are hundreds of ways to wait.

Babysit a neighbor's child, pull crabgrass, add weight,
then diet, play tennis, pretend you never knew
a figure beckons from the spirit gate.

Work out, pay bills, call old friends, cultivate
new ones, design your garden in red, white, and blue.
There are hundreds of ways to wait.

Tutor for literacy, draw, paint, meditate,
work eight hours straight, make lists. Whatever you do,
a figure beckons from the spirit gate.

Whatever you do, don't stop or hesitate.
Grill sea bass on the deck, raise a glass or two.
There are hundreds of ways to wait.
A figure beckons from the spirit gate.

Lines Carried by Wind

Wind marks on the sand
by morning they are gone
Witch's secrets in my dream
linger like a song

        See the woman walking there
        Sand stirs, whirls, streams like smoke
        stings her legs in needle bites
        Still she walks, facing the wind
        facing into the wind, meeting the wind
        A masthead set above the waves

Wind marks on the sand
by morning they are gone
Witch's pleasures in my dream
linger like a song

        See the woman walking there
        her silver hair a flag of silk
        Her laughter rides the wind
        her skin cleaned of artifice and tears
        October wind renders its own
        leaves no trace

Wind marks on the sand
by morning they are gone
Witch's secrets in my dream
linger like a song

        See the woman walking there
        She watches blackbirds loop and rise
        iridescent as desire
        Sanderlings scout the edge,
        poke and run, discrete
        She resumes her pace into the wind

What Is Held Back
for Jo

Reports from the islands
are washing ashore, not in a bottle.
This sorrow, like nitrogen, eighty percent
of the air we breathe, now as liquid,
surges like a geyser from your core,
pierces your mantle with such cold
it will burn through the crust, furious
to surface, sloughing willed controls
like so many unsightly warts.
After it subsides, and it will,
to ordinary vapor, you'll recognize
the pain and, in time, new skin.

Watch then who swims ashore
from the underground river
where she hides deep
in the cave of your mind:
the child you were, invisible
as the shape of water
because the one in charge
allows no other.

It's time to see again
the tall thin girl, full of sauce,
who calls out, "Ready or not,
here I come." She's ready
for jump rope hot pepper,
ready for Bultmann or Tillich.
She'll speak out, stand up
and say what she sees.
Welcome this child,
ready to touch the ground
of your being, and hand you
her gift of courage.

A Story Is About Something

the way a string is wound
around a stick. You think
you have yourself
a ball of string, but if
you locate one end
and roll it out, you'll find
the center, small, made of cedar,
a line used in another season
to launch a kite and anchor it.

A story might have to be about
something, but you could like
a peach for its own juicy taste
and not for the hard brain
at its center. A few red
strands clinging to the stone
you might examine
while the taste of summer lingers
in your mouth.

A story might be a nest
built from twigs and hair,
wind-thrust downy weed
pieced and wound about
dappled memory and need.
The wren returns to an old china dish
in the garage. Although
it's been moved twice,
she finds her way through
a broken window and behind
the truck to build her nest.
Story is not the dish,
but what she brings.
And it does not end there.

Sue Lile Inman was born in Little Rock, Arkansas. She received her B.A. in English from Agnes Scott College in 1958 and her M.A. from Clemson University in 1978. She has taught in the English Departments of Clemson University and Furman University. She now leads writing workshops, does free-lance editing, and writes. Her publications, other than poetry, include articles and stories in *Southern Living Classics*, *Southern Accents*, *The Arts Journal*, *Artscene*, and *The South Carolina Review*, among others. With the exception of a year spent in Japan, she and her husband have lived in Greenville, South Carolina, since 1963. They have four children and two grandchildren.